IN THE
ALLEYS

PHOTOGRAPHS BY GODFREY FRANKEL

TEXT BY LAURA GOLDSTEIN

FOREWORD BY GORDON PARKS

SMITHSONIAN INSTITUTION PRESS ◆ WASHINGTON AND LONDON

IN THE
ALLEYS

KIDS IN THE SHADOW
OF THE CAPITOL

Acquiring editor: Amy Pastan
Production editor: Jack Kirshbaum
Designer: Kathleen Sims
Production Manager: Kenneth J. Sabol
Hand Lettering: Alfonzo Dennis Garner, Jr.

Library of Congress Catalog-in-Publication Data

Frankel, Godfrey.
In the alleys : kids in the shadow of the Capitol / photographs by
Godfrey Frankel ; text by Laura Goldstein ; foreword by Gordon Parks.
p.   cm.
Includes bibliographical references.
ISBN 1-56098-536-4 (cloth : alk. paper); 1-56098-663-8 (pbk : alk. paper)
1. Afro-American children—Washington (D.C.)—Portraits.   2. Afro-
Americans—Washington (D.C.)—Social conditions—Pictorial works.
3. Afro-Americans—Social conditions—To 1964—Pictorial works.
4. Washington (D.C.)—Social conditions—Pictorial works.   5. Frankel, Godfrey.
I. Goldstein, Laura.   II. Title.
TR681.C5F72   1995
779′.930523′089960730753—dc20   95-14993

British Library Cataloging-in-Publication data available

00   99   98   97   96   95   5   4   3   2   1

Manufactured in Hong Kong

♾ The paper used in this publication meets the minimum requirements of the American National
Standard for Permanence of Paper for Printed Library Materials Z39.48-1984.

Jacket illustration: Photo by Godfrey Frankel.

For permission to reproduce any of the illustrations, correspond directly with the author. The
Smithsonian Institution Press does not retain reproduction rights for these illustrations individually or
maintain a file of addresses for photo sources.

CONTENTS

FOREWORD

Some memories, more jarring than others, push my thoughts back
through time. Then what I remember comes howling back with
things I should have known, even though I didn't know they existed.
Godfrey Frankel's photographs of black street kids offer me a window
to a bothersome memory I failed to escape.

Autumn had arrived. I was in Washington for the first time, moving
eagerly in the midpoint of a morning turned honey and amber. The
Capitol was standing quiet and strong at one end of the mall, the Lin-
coln Memorial at the other. It was a fine day for walking, and my camera's eye, caught up in the stately corridors of the city, led me along the
Mall, then southward toward the banks of the Potomac. As I walked
on, the morning gradually began to take on gloom. A weariness began
to set in. Then suddenly I was moving in an arena that had rippled into
existence with such hardness it shook me. A crowded trash-littered
street paved of aged brick and enclosed by a maze of gloomy alleys.
Smoke curled into the air over long lines of squalid brick tenements. Trucks screeched, dogs barked, eyes clouded with despair

stared through grimy windows. But, for me, the most intense presence in this dirty disgruntled place was that of black children. One group sat on a stone curb, mesmerized by smoke curling upward from a bonfire. Poorly clothed, some romped about in a way that seemed to have no purpose other than to keep themselves warm. Others walked the endless alleys, silently disappearing into the shadows. I had entered Washington's Southwest quadrant, where eventually my camera would grow to know this dark part of the nation's capital in its own way. A year later, in 1943, Godfrey Frankel would melt into the same desolation and put his camera to work.

Fifty years and more have passed since then. Now I am told that enough laws were bunched together to give death to this terrible place—that bit by bit the "Island," as it was called by its inhabitants, was eventually scratched from the city's geography. Nevertheless, that festering space, once so close to the White House, still haunts my memory, still lingers sadly in the faces of those children, who became poetry for Godfrey Frankel's camera. Their houses there are numberless and doorless now. Hopefully most of them survived to live as woman and man—safely away from where their lives took root.

Gordon Parks
November 28, 1994

PREFACE AND ACKNOWLEDGMENTS

In the fall of 1992, Linton Weeks, then my editor at the *Washington Post Magazine,* dropped a packet of old black-and-white photographs on my desk. They had been shot in and around Washington's poorest neighborhoods—the inhabited alleys of Southwest D.C.—some fifty years earlier. He thought the photos, images of children at play on the secluded alley streets, were intriguing and wanted to publish them in an upcoming issue. "The photographer's still around; he lives out in Silver Spring," he told me. "Why don't you go talk to him and see what he has to say?"

A few days later I paid a visit to Godfrey and Lillian Frankel in their 1950s-modern house on a quiet, tree-lined street in a suburb ten miles from downtown Washington. Both retired, they live amid a comfortable clutter of books, plants, artworks, and family photographs. Lillian, I learned over tea and cookies, is a poet; Godfrey had been a social worker for the government and spent nearly twenty years as a program adviser. His last assignment was with the National Institute on Drug Abuse.

The first thing that struck me about Godfrey—bowled me over, really—was his youthfulness. At an age when most people are slowing down, Godfrey, then in his late seventies, was gearing up for a whole new enterprise. Though an accomplished amateur photographer with works in several museum collections, he had never had time, through the long years of building a career and raising a family, to concentrate on promoting his art. Now he was giving it his full attention—sifting through a half-century's worth of negatives piled up in the basement, cataloging, printing, taking his best pictures around to local dealers. The effort had paid off: at the time of our initial meeting, he was spending hours in the darkroom, making prints for an exhibit of some of his alley photographs at a prominent Washington gallery, their first-ever public showing.

The fact that we were nearly fifty years apart in age, or that I was a stranger—and a reporter no less—didn't put a crimp in conversation as it sometimes does. We talked for hours. Making the alley photographs in 1943 had deeply affected Godfrey, and he was eager to share the lessons he had learned. The alleys, he explained, were "hidden" neighborhoods, tucked back behind broad city streets, where people crowded into ramshackle dwellings that lacked even the most basic amenities—electricity, heat, running water. By experiencing first-hand the society forged in the face of such poverty and isolation, he told me, he had gained a greater appreciation for the meaning of "community" and a deeper understanding of its importance in people's lives. I was not surprised when he went on to say that the same impulse that directed him to the alleys in the first place—concern for the plight of the residents—subsequently led him to leave a job in journalism, set aside his camera, and embark on a forty-year career in social work. We talked about that decision, a difficult one for him to make at the time, and whether he had any regrets. We talked about the creative process, and having faith in one's work, and his surprise and delight at being "discovered" at the age of 79. I listened for clues, trying to glean wisdom from this man who had lived a long, productive, and seemingly satisfied life, and still had new adventures on the horizon.

When I got back to the office, I was practically bursting. I had more than enough information to write the story my editor wanted. The article, titled "Street Kids," appeared in the *Washington Post Magazine* on December 20, 1992. Within days, Godfrey's phone started ringing. People who had grown up in Southwest called to share their recollections, or to identify friends and relatives in the pictures. I began receiving letters at the newspaper from people who had read the article and wanted to know where they could go to see more of Godfrey's work, or perhaps buy a book of his photographs.

A handful of books about the alleys exist, but most are academic studies or government pamphlets dating from the turn of the century and focusing on the problems of housing and sanitation. Though the neighborhoods in the pictures are long gone—lost to the forces of "urban renewal" during the late 1950s—what we heard from former residents is that their memories remain strong, and their attachment to the communities of their childhood stronger still. That got us to thinking: before the people too are gone, we decided, we would talk to them about what they remembered and cherished of the old Southwest, and use their words to add another dimension to Godfrey's artistic vision.

We spent the next ten months interviewing dozens of former Southwest residents for this project; some had lived in the alleys, others on the surrounding streets. We looked for people who would have been children in 1943, when the photographs were made. Though scattered throughout the metropolitan area, Southwesters maintain strong ties, and we rarely left an interview without the names of one or two friends to contact. We showed subjects the pictures and tape-recorded their comments; we also spoke with local historians, academics, sociologists, and others who have studied or written about Washington's inhabited alleys. Together, their accounts form the basis for the text that accompanies the photographs.

Godfrey and I continue to spend many hours talking. I am grateful to him for inviting me into this project, and for his generosity of time and spirit. Many other people made this book possible. My thanks to Linton Weeks and Deborah Needleman for the original assignment;

Charles E. Banks, James G. Banks, Lawrence E. Boone, Clementine Buchanan, Joseph Owen Curtis, Thomas Fields, Ernestine Ford, Medell E. Ford, Lillian Jones, Phyllis Martin, Hilton O. Overton Jr., Roberta Patrick, Nathaniel Price, Linda Scott, Miles Scott, Howard Stone, Daniel Thursz, Princess D. Whitfield, and Henry Williams for allowing me to interview them and use their voices in the preparation of the manuscript; George Hemphill and Kathleen Ewing for their input on the photographs; Delores Smith for access to source materials from the documentary film *Southwest Remembered;* the staffs of the Washingtoniana Room of the Martin Luther King Jr. Library, the Southwest Branch of the D.C. Public Library, and the Historical Society of Washington, D.C.; my *Washington Post* colleagues John Cotter, Deborah Fleming, Peter Perl, and Michael Stuntz for their thoughtful reading of the text; Amy Pastan and Jack Kirshbaum of Smithsonian Institution Press for their care and encouragement; Lillian Frankel for all the lunches; and my family and friends for their patience and support.

—*Laura Goldstein*

NOTES FROM THE PHOTOGRAPHER

In 1982 I retired from federal employment. Long before, I had set myself a goal of bringing my photographic collection up to a level where I could show prints to galleries and museums. I organized my negatives into subject areas, brushed up on laboratory technique, and made new prints of pictures taken years earlier in Washington and New York—a project that was forty years in the making.

When I began showing my work to galleries in the mid-1980s, few were featuring documentary or street photography. The Corcoran Gallery in Washington was the first to collect my photographs, followed by the National Museum of American Art. Then, in 1987, George Hemphill presented my first solo show of New York pictures at Middendorf Gallery in Washington, where he was then director of photography. In 1990 Howard Greenberg agreed to represent me in

New York, and in 1992 the Kathleen Ewing Gallery in Washington exhibited, for the first time, my alley dwelling photographs.

The possibility of a book was first suggested to me by Richard Rowson, director of publishing at the Woodrow Wilson Center Press, who had viewed my prints at the Ewing Gallery. He proved instrumental in helping to develop what eventually became the proposal for this book.

Some time later, Amy Pastan of Smithsonian Institution Press called me after seeing the feature on my work that had run in the *Washington Post Magazine*. She initiated this project, and shepherded it through to completion with grace and good nature.

Selecting pictures for the book gave me a nostalgic pleasure, allowing me to relive the days I had spent discovering the alley dwellings, riding through the neighborhood on my bicycle, and watching the children as they played games, laughed, and called out to me.

To the above individuals I am deeply grateful, and to the following, I wish to express my sincere thanks for their contributions.

First of all, to Laura Goldstein, who did such an excellent job in the preparation of the text and, in addition, was so good to work with; Stuart Diekmeyer, photographer and superb master printer, who assisted me in printing the photographs; Morgan Frankel, attorney for the U.S. Senate, for his critical analysis and understanding; Jane Van Nimmen of the Prints and Photographs Division of the Library of Congress; Tom Beck, curator of the Albin O. Kuhn Library and Gallery at the University of Maryland, Baltimore County; Margaret Feldman, Ph.D., Southwest Washington civic leader; Jerome S. Paige, provost of the University of Baltimore; James I. Ballard Jr., photographer and curator of the archives of the D.C. Department of Public and Assisted Housing; Howard Gillette, Ph.D., professor of American Studies at George Washington University; and Lillian Frankel, my wife, whose fresh eyes and creative sense in art, writing, and life have always been a source of strength to me in all my endeavors.

—*Godfrey Frankel*

TO MY WIFE, LILLIAN,
AND SONS, STEPHEN AND DANIEL,
FOR GIVING ME COURAGE, SUPPORT, AND HUMOR
BEFORE AND DURING THE WRITING OF THIS BOOK—
AND TO THE ALLEY DWELLERS,
WHO ENDURED THE DAILY HARDSHIP.

IN THE ALLEYS
THE
PHOTOGRAPHS OF
GODFREY FRANKEL

◆ ◆ ◆

"ABANDON YE ALL HOPE
WHO ENTERS THE ALLEY COMMUNITY SHOWN IN THE DIAGRAM ALONE
AFTER DARK. THIS IS A TYPICAL INHABITED ALLEY, WITH ITS MAZE OF
ALLEYS OFF ALLEYS, EACH ONE LINED WITH SQUALID HOUSES—
A HIDDEN VILLAGE OF 33 DWELLINGS."

—FROM THE FILES OF
WASHINGTON'S ALLEY DWELLING AUTHORITY, 1933

*T*he year is 1943, and Washington is a city at war. A young man, newly arrived from his home in Cleveland, Ohio, buys a bicycle to get around because gas rationing and other shortages have made transportation difficult. He has come to town for a job, but he doesn't have to be at work—reporting on the capital's nightlife for the *Washington Daily News*—until after dark. So while waiting for night to fall, he carries his bicycle down the narrow flight of stairs leading from his second-floor apartment at Seventeenth and I streets Northwest and heads off to explore, no particular destination in mind. A novice photographer, he slings his Super Ikonta BX around his neck and tucks a few spare rolls of film in his jacket pocket. If I'm lucky, he thinks, maybe I'll find some fresh material to shoot.

He pedals off in the direction of the White House a few blocks away, then down Fourteenth Street to Constitution Avenue, past the neat rows of temporary federal office buildings arrayed with military precision along the broad expanse of the National Mall. Crossing the Mall and continuing south, he heads toward the Potomac River waterfront, following the curve of the Washington Channel as it runs along Maine Avenue, past fishing boats and bustling seafood houses, past wholesale produce trucks unloading their daily cargo of fruits and vegetables, until he finds himself in new and unfamiliar surroundings.

He has arrived in the city's Southwest quadrant, a short distance from where he started in miles, but far removed in terms of the lives of its people. Here, in an area long referred to by residents as "the Island" because of its waterside location and relative isolation from the rest of the capital, little of "official" Washington is evident. The crowded streets, paved in crumbling brick and crammed with corner stores, food markets, drugstores, barbershops, bars, and warehouses, are shabbier. The houses, some with battered wooden stoops and wire gates on rusted hinges, are more dilapidated. The inhabitants are noticeably poorer, and most of them are black.

Walking his bicycle now, the photographer spies activity in the middle of a block, people coming and going from a narrow passageway tucked between two buildings. Curious about what lies beyond, he follows them, steering a path down a walkway barely wide enough for two adults to pass through at once. When he emerges on the other side, he comes face to face with the material he is looking for.

"THE ARTIST'S TASK IS NOT TO ALTER THE WORLD AS THE EYE SEES IT INTO A WORLD OF AESTHETIC REALITY, BUT TO PERCEIVE THE AESTHETIC REALITY WITHIN THE ACTUAL WORLD, AND TO MAKE AN UNDISTURBED AND FAITHFUL RECORD OF THE INSTANT IN WHICH THIS MOVEMENT OF CREATIVENESS ACHIEVES ITS MOST EXPRESSIVE CRYSTALLIZATION."[1]
—JAMES AGEE, *A WAY OF SEEING*

Godfrey Frankel had discovered Washington's inhabited alleys, labyrinthine warrens lined with dreary dwellings where the city's poor people lived. These hidden enclaves—viewed as breeding grounds for crime, disease, and despair—had been a target of housing reform efforts almost since their beginnings a century earlier. By 1943, when he first encountered them, the alleys of Southwest D.C. were home to as many as 10,000 residents.[2]

"I was amazed when I first saw these alley houses—monotonous, drab, two-story brick dwellings stretching a block long, and people spilling out of the doorways directly into the street," the photographer remembers. He'd never seen anything like it back home in Ohio. "Cleveland had plenty of substandard housing, deprivation, and poverty. But these Washington dwellings were different. They compacted the oppressed population into rows of buildings sandwiched between streets of better housing with regular sidewalks, curbs, trees, and lawns."

Whereas conventional houses faced out toward the public streets, the alley dwellings were enclosed within the interiors of blocks,

◆ ◆ ◆

THE HEART OF THE SOUTHWEST:
FOURTH AND I STREETS, 1939.

PHOTOGRAPH COPYRIGHT
JOSEPH OWEN CURTIS.

◆　◆　◆

FRAME HOUSES ALONG LOWER
FOURTH STREET.

PHOTOGRAPH COPYRIGHT
JOSEPH OWEN CURTIS.

◆ ◆ ◆

VIEW OF ALLEY DWELLINGS OFF NORTH
CAPITOL STREET, NOVEMBER 1935.

PHOTOGRAPH BY CARL M. MYDANS.
(LIBRARY OF CONGRESS COLLECTIONS)

◆ ◆ ◆

INSIDE NAYLOR'S ALLEY, JANUARY 1936.

(ALLEY DWELLING AUTHORITY PHOTOGRAPH,
D.C. DEPARTMENT OF PUBLIC
AND ASSISTED HOUSING)

shielded from view behind high fences and rows of rickety wooden sheds. A typical "blind alley"—so called because the only access was through a narrow passageway leading out to the sidewalk—might contain a dozen or more dwellings, opening onto an alley some thirty feet across.[3] Typically two stories high and made of brick or wood, the houses were cramped and dark inside. Most contained four small rooms: a living room and kitchen downstairs, two bedrooms upstairs. Often two families shared a single dwelling, one on each level; sometimes as many as a dozen people occupied a single room.

There were as many as two hundred such alleys scattered throughout the city, primarily in the part of Northwest known today as Foggy Bottom, and in Southwest, the area bounded by the Mall, South Capitol Street, the Anacostia River, and the Washington Channel. They were called by fanciful names—Willow Tree Alley, Pleasant Court, Golden Street, Broad Alley, Tin Cup Alley, Temperance Court—but the evocative nicknames hardly did justice to the deplorable living conditions. According to accounts of the time, as recently as 1950 more than 20 percent of Southwest's 5,600 alley dwellings had no electricity, and more than 70 percent no central heating; residents relied on oil lamps for light and coal or woodstoves for warmth.[4] Few had indoor plumbing; water came instead from a pump behind the house. And, in what has become the most enduring symbol of the alley's deprivation, the majority of the dwellings had outdoor toilets. The picture of outhouses in the shadow of the Capitol remains, for many, the defining image of Old Southwest Washington.

Frankel was moved. Wandering through the alleys, he couldn't help but feel as though he had entered another world—"inside someplace and between someplace," he says. "There was a specialness to it. Because of the physical nature of the place, it carried a different character." That "special" quality emerged in the face of obvious hardship: most of the people who lived in the alleys did so because they could not afford to live anywhere else. But despite the harsh conditions, it was a community just the same. Parents raised their children, men and women went off to work, lovers quarreled, friends played, neighbors protected one another.

◆ ◆ ◆

A FAMILY INSIDE A DWELLING
AT 409 I STREET S.E. 1939.

(ALLEY DWELLING AUTHORITY PHOTOGRAPH,
D.C. DEPARTMENT OF PUBLIC
AND ASSISTED HOUSING)

◆ ◆ ◆

INTERIOR OF A DWELLING ON
GOLDEN STREET S.W., DECEMBER 1941.
A STEAMER TRUNK DOUBLES AS A BED;
A STOVE PROVIDES THE ONLY HEAT.

(ALLEY DWELLING AUTHORITY PHOTOGRAPH,
D.C. DEPARTMENT OF PUBLIC AND ASSISTED HOUSING)

◆ ◆ ◆

LAUNDRY DAY,
DELAWARE AND I STREETS S.W., 1948.

PHOTOGRAPH COPYRIGHT
JOSEPH OWEN CURTIS

AN OUTHOUSE, THE MOST OFT-CITED SYMBOL
OF THE ALLEYS' DEPRIVATION.

(D.C. DEPARTMENT OF PUBLIC AND ASSISTED HOUSING)

♦ ♦ ♦

AN ALLEY AT B-AND-A-HALF STREET S.W.,
WITH THE SOCIAL SECURITY BUILDING
(NOW HEALTH AND HUMAN SERVICES)
IN THE BACKGROUND, MARCH 1951.

(D.C. DEPARTMENT OF PUBLIC AND ASSISTED HOUSING)

In the weeks that followed, Frankel returned to the alleys again and again, capturing on film the everyday lives of the people who lived there. By his own admission, he must have been a curious sight—a slightly built, bespectacled white man walking the streets of a segregated community, camera in hand. But over time, he became a familiar presence. "There was always a question, 'What's this guy doing in our neighborhood?'" he says, then offers this answer: "He's a friendly guy, he's part crazy, he's taking pictures."

"I WANTED TO SHOW THE THINGS THAT HAD TO BE CORRECTED. I WANTED TO SHOW THE THINGS THAT HAD TO BE APPRECIATED."[5]
—AMERICAN PHOTOGRAPHER LEWIS HINE (1874–1940)

At first, Frankel viewed the alleys as a place where his photographs could move people to action. Like camera-wielding reformers before him—Lewis Hine, for example, whose pictures of Ellis Island immigrants and children at work in southern textile mills in the early 1900s earned him the title of "the great documenter of social justice in America"[6]—Frankel wanted to show the things that had to be corrected. But, like Hine, he also wanted to show the things of value.

For the alleys, he soon discovered, were far from the hopeless, amoral places their reputation made them out to be. They were thriving neighborhoods, each with its own cast of characters, social mores, and support systems. "Even though my initial motive was to reveal inadequate housing, poverty, and squalor, there was something else I was seeing too," Frankel recalls. "Something precious was coming out of this sordid environment. I attempted to capture it."

He was drawn most of all to the children, who spent the long, hot summer afternoons at play on the alley streets. In the photographer's eyes, their activities lent "an aura of mystery" to the otherwise squalid surroundings. The alley—trash-strewn and unsightly though it may have been—was transformed by their youthful imaginations into a castle, a fort, a raging battlefield. "As I stood and watched them play, I

◆ ◆ ◆

ELLIS ISLAND IMMIGRANTS, 1908.

PHOTOGRAPH BY LEWIS HINE.
(PHOTOGRAPHY COLLECTIONS, UNIVERSITY OF
MARYLAND BALTIMORE COUNTY)

♦ ♦ ♦

CHILD LABORER IN A
NORTH CAROLINA COTTON MILL, 1908–9

PHOTOGRAPH BY LEWIS HINE.
(PHOTOGRAPHY COLLECTIONS, UNIVERSITY OF
MARYLAND BALTIMORE COUNTY)

couldn't help but think how the innocence of childhood somehow has a way of protecting them from a brutal environment. I felt the dignity and strength of these children," he says, "and I tried to show it in my photos."

In the images of children jumping rope, playing cops and robbers, racing one another across the cobblestones, we see something of the essence of childhood. We see, as photographer Helen Levitt did on the streets of New York's Harlem, that "life in a ghetto can have moments of pure fantasy."[7] When Frankel spots a group of kids playing a ragtag game of "let's pretend," it doesn't matter that the young superheroes' capes are made of threadbare towels and their masks of ragged cloth. To be sure, reminders of poverty are everywhere—boys and girls in hand-me-down clothes with sleeves that are too long or too short, or wearing boots in the summertime, perhaps the only shoes they had—but the hardship fades in the face of youthful ebullience.

In its compassion and directness, Frankel's style owes something to the social documentarians of the 1930s and 1940s, especially those working to capture the faces of America's urban and rural poor for the federal Farm Security Administration. The images of factory workers and sharecroppers, farm mothers and migrant laborers made famous by Walker Evans, Dorothea Lange, and others were just beginning to work their way into the American consciousness, getting widespread exposure in newspapers and magazines. Nor was Frankel the only one to turn his camera on the alleys: at roughly the same time, such well-known FSA photographers as Edwin Rosskam, Gordon Parks, and Carl Mydans were dispatched to make a formal record of alley conditions. Though Frankel was influenced by those images, his photographs are nonetheless intensely personal documents. Working independently, he was compelled to make them by his desire to form an emotional connection with his subjects, rather than by the need to meet the demands of an assignment. "I really believe that the reason we take certain pictures is far deeper than we permit ourselves to consider," he suggests, "and the process of making art is more involved and complicated."

◆ ◆ ◆

MIGRANT WORKERS IN CALIFORNIA,
FEBRUARY 1936.

PHOTOGRAPH BY DOROTHEA LANGE.
(LIBRARY OF CONGRESS COLLECTIONS)

♦ ♦ ♦

A YOUNG GIRL INSIDE HER HOME
NEAR THE CAPITOL, JUNE 1942.

PHOTOGRAPH BY GORDON R. PARKS.
(LIBRARY OF CONGRESS COLLECTIONS)

◆ ◆ ◆

KITCHEN IN FLOYD BURROUGHS HOME,
HALE COUNTY, ALABAMA, SUMMER 1936.

PHOTOGRAPH BY WALKER EVANS. (LIBRARY OF
CONGRESS COLLECTIONS)

Frankel began to conceive of the alleys as his studio, learning where the light emanated from at different times of the day, how the late-afternoon sun modeled the brick pavements and house fronts, how the eyes of the children shone in the twilight. He kept his equipment to a minimum—just a medium-format camera and a couple of extra rolls of film; no filters, no special lenses. Like Frenchman Henri Cartier-Bresson, one of the earliest practitioners of street photography, Frankel was less concerned with "making art" than with revealing the drama of everyday life. He practiced what photo historian Jane Livingston terms "the aesthetic of imperfection"—rejecting polished technique in favor of unvarnished reality.[8] "The camera was to be incidental," he explains. "It was merely an instrument that recorded what my eyes saw."

Frankel worked informally, never setting up his shots but waiting patiently for the right moment to click the shutter. He would stand in the background while the children played around him, sometimes waiting for so long that they would notice him and stiffen up or start to mug for the camera, and the natural image he wanted would be lost. Other times, the pictures found him. One day he turned a corner and stumbled on half a dozen children planted like sentries along the front step of an alley market (p. 65). Their faces are a gallery of childhood emotions: curiosity, shyness, fear, youthful disregard; from the middle of the group, a boy stares out defiantly, a fierce challenge in his four-year-old eyes. "Sometimes you just come upon the right picture. It's there! And you shoot without waiting," Frankel says. "You shoot again, and you just know you have it. Everything is right—light, subject, mood, composition."

Frankel made some of his most affecting photos in the late afternoons, as the waning sun threw shadows across the pavement. That is when we see a little boy dancing alone, his tiny figure afloat on a sea of bricks (p. 62). The light scales across the building behind him, catching the edges of the door and window and framing him in parallel lines of light. Long shadows mark the ground beside him, but we can't see who casts them. There is at once a sweetness and a sense of foreboding, as in a De Chirico painting come to life. Curator Beaumont Newhall, who included this image in a show at the Museum of Modern Art in 1946, said of it, "The lens will hint at the unknown, the subtle, the unclassified, and that of which we have little knowledge. The child in the picture looks and wonders and that expression is never lost."[9]

Many of the children in Frankel's photos appear poised on the cusp of adolescence, caught between unknowing fantasy and the stark reality of life in the alley. We see it in the pose of a boy who stands with his hands thrust in his pockets and a faraway look in his eyes (p. 43). His shirt and shorts are dirty, his little-man's shoes scuffed and untied. Though only a child, he carries himself with an air of maturity beyond his years, as if by passing through the open gate behind him he has suddenly entered the world of grownups. We see the same attitude again in a photo of two boys shoulder-to-shoulder in front of a house (p. 73), their open stances and confrontational gazes nearly identical, but for the fact that the smaller of the two has his thumb stuck in his mouth—a poignant reminder that these little guardians are just children after all.

Occasionally Frankel would join in the play, or hand over his camera so the kids could peek through the viewfinder. Sometimes he would return with photographs from a previous session. The children began to look forward to his visits. "When I missed a week, they would say, 'We were looking for you,'" he remembers. "They greeted me when I came into the alley. Even their parents would ask, 'Where were you? The kids missed you.'" This familiarity gives his photos of children and adults alike a remarkable measure of intimacy. When two women lean out neighboring windows to talk (p. 51), or pass time together on a cement stoop (p. 38), we can almost hear the stories they tell. Unguarded moments speak loudest: in one particularly eloquent image, a middle-aged woman gazes from a second-story window, her arms crossed against her chest, her shoulder sagging against the edge of the window frame (p. 53). She allows herself the hint of a shy smile—perhaps the photographer has just paid her a compliment from the street below. Like an Edward Hopper painting, the photo illustrates something of the fundamental challenge of human existence, the weariness that comes from facing an uphill climb day after day.

Frankel is sensitive to arguments that he exploited or stereotyped his subjects; his objective, he says, was simply to tell a story about people—to capture what was genuine and unique about alley community and to subvert expectations of what life in a slum is really like. For in the slum there is caring and safety as well as danger, happiness and freedom along with misfortune—much as in any other place. "Art and beauty," the photographer says, "can be everywhere."

"THEY DESTROYED A COMMUNITY, I MEAN A REAL COMMUNITY. IT WAS LIKE A LITTLE SMALL SOUTHERN TOWN. YOU'LL NEVER FIND THAT KIND OF HISTORY AGAIN IN WASHINGTON, D.C."[10]

—FORMER RESIDENT OF DIXON COURT, THE CITY'S LARGEST INHABITED ALLEY

Viewed from the perspective of half a century later, Frankel's photographs take on an added significance. For not long after the pictures were made, the alleys would be gone forever, wiped out in a 1950s program of large-scale urban renewal (see p. 91). Today, little of Old Southwest remains, save for a handful of churches, schools, and historic homes. The children in the photos, now adults in their fifties and sixties, have no tangible history to show their own children, no landmarks, no playgrounds—nothing except photographs and memories of a long established and once thriving, if easily dismissed, community. "They considered our place as being kind of blighted," observes one child of the alleys, today the principal of a junior high school in Washington, D.C. "I never understood, because it's the place where I experienced the greatest feeling of love."[11]

The vast majority of people who were displaced when the wrecking ball tore through Southwest in the late 1950s were able to move into better housing, but many nonetheless lamented the loss of their neighborhoods. For Frankel too, the impact of watching the dissolution of a community he had come to know was profound and long-lasting. Still fresh from his time in the alleys, in 1945 Frankel left Washington for Cleveland and a job with the federal War Relocation Authority, the organization responsible for resettling Japanese Americans who had been held in internment camps after the bombing of Pearl Harbor during World War II. Though he was using his camera professionally for the first time, producing brochures and pamphlets for the agency, it was during a stint at the Heart Mountain Relocation Center in Wyoming that Frankel began to think differently about his future. As a photographer, he thought, he might be able to earn a living—if he were lucky—but he would have to put commerce before art and take pictures of whatever his bosses wanted him to. As a social worker, he could live by his humanitarian convictions, be guaranteed a steady income, and continue to pursue photography as he wished. When the relocation agency completed its work at the end of the year, Frankel resolved to enroll in graduate school at Columbia University for a master's degree in social work.

The decision was not an easy one. When he arrived in New York, one of the first things he did was pay a visit to Alfred Stieglitz in his midtown Manhattan gallery. Stieglitz, the dean of New York photographers, praised his work and encouraged him to show it to Beaumont Newhall, then curator of photography at the Museum of Modern Art. That led to the inclusion of several alley pictures in two group shows at the museum, in 1946 and again in 1948. At the same time, Frankel embarked on another project: while waiting for the school term to begin, he spent his days prowling the sidewalks of Manhattan's Lower East Side, taking pictures of the ethnic writings in store windows, the ornate ironwork of the Third Avenue Elevated train, concrete friezes carved into tenement exteriors, and "street furniture" of all kinds. Like the Washington pictures, Frankel's New York photos are informed by his interest in people and the environments in which they live. But to a greater extent than the earlier work, they also reveal a keen eye for design and composition—what he calls the "archaeology" of the city landscape.

He joined the Photo League, an influential social-action camera club, where he met like-minded artists. When time came to start school in 1948, he hesitated. "I had ambivalent feelings," he recalls. "The problem was, should I stick at photography? I was getting a hold

◆　◆　◆

WAR RELOCATION AUTHORITY CENTER,
HEART MOUNTAIN, WYOMING,
JULY 1945.

PHOTOGRAPH BY GODFREY FRANKEL.

♦ ♦ ♦

WAR RELOCATION AUTHORITY CENTER,
HEART MOUNTAIN, WYOMING,
JULY 1945.

PHOTOGRAPH BY GODFREY FRANKEL.

◆ ◆ ◆

THIRD AVENUE ELEVATED LOOKING
SOUTH, NEW YORK CITY, 1947.

PHOTOGRAPH BY GODFREY FRANKEL.

ELEVATED STATION HOUSE WINDOW,
NEW YORK CITY, 1947.

PHOTOGRAPH BY GODFREY FRANKEL.

♦ ♦ ♦

STREET POET IN SPANISH HARLEM,
NEW YORK CITY, 1947.

PHOTOGRAPH BY GODFREY FRANKEL.

on it. Important people like Stieglitz and Alexey Brodovitch [art director of *Harper's Bazaar*] were encouraging me. But it was a matter of
waiting for the phone to ring and hoping for some kind of opportunity, as against going into an endeavor like social work, where I felt
comfortable—just as comfortable, I suppose—with more structure
and regularity." He was a newlywed and would soon have two young
sons to support. In the end, he opted for security, and the rewards of a
career spent in pursuit of other ambitions no less dearly held. "It
was tough for me for a while," he says, then pauses to consider the
path taken. "I'm glad I made that choice. There are other kicks I got
out of life. . . . I probably did more as a social worker than as a
photographer."

Today, at 82, Frankel lives with his wife of fifty years, the poet Lillian
Frankel, in Silver Spring, Maryland. It was not until 1982, when he
retired after twenty years as a public health adviser for the federal government, that he blew the dust off the hundreds of photos he had made
decades earlier. His nostalgia-laden images tapped a burgeoning interest in the documentarians of the 1930s and 1940s, and galleries in
Washington, New York, and San Francisco soon "discovered" him. In
the intervening years, photography had come into its own, both as a
legitimate art form and a popular medium. In 1992—nearly fifty years
after their creation—the alley photographs had their first full public
exhibition, something the photographer himself never imagined
when he set off on that long-ago bicycle ride.

Note to readers: The photographs on the following pages were taken in and around
the inhabited alleys of Southwest Washington, and in some cases other sections of
the city, in 1943. The accompanying words, unaltered, are those of former
Southwest residents interviewed in 1993 and 1994 (credits on p. 99).

31

SOUTHWEST PEOPLE WERE VERY CLOSE. THEY WOULD FIGHT AND SQUABBLE, LIKE FAMILIES

DO, BUT WHEN PUSH CAME TO SHOVE THEY WOULD STICK TOGETHER. IT'S HARD, IN

RETROSPECT, LOOKING AT THESE PICTURES, TO SEE WHERE WE CAME FROM.

WE'VE COME A PRETTY LONG WAY.

SOUTHWEST WAS NOT A GOOD PLACE TO LIVE, TO OUTSIDERS. IT WAS BEST NOT TO TELL

THEM YOU WERE FROM SOUTHWEST. THE FIRST THING THEY THOUGHT OF WERE THE

ALLEYS. IF YOU LIVED IN AN ALLEY, YOU WERE CALLED "ALLEY RAT" ON TOP OF

EVERYTHING ELSE. IT LEFT YOU FEELING BAD. THE ONLY PROTECTION YOU HAD WAS TO

GET BACK HOME TO THE ALLEYS, WHERE YOU WERE SAFE.

ON SATURDAY NIGHTS YOU'D HEAR PEOPLE DRINKING, AND THE MUSIC, THEY'D

PLAY THE BLUES A LOT. AND YOU'D HAVE SOME WHO WOULD FIGHT—

THEY'D REALLY FIGHT—BUT YOU NEVER HAD THE VIOLENCE, AT LEAST I DIDN'T SEE IT. . . .

CHILDREN STAYED IN CHILDREN'S PLACES.

THERE WAS AN INTIMACY ABOUT LIVING IN THE ALLEY. THE ONLY PLACE PEOPLE HAD TO
GO WAS OUT ON THE FRONT. AND, OF COURSE, THEY CAME TO KNOW EACH OTHER
AND KNOW EACH OTHER'S BUSINESS. AND NO ONE HAD VERY MUCH. BUT IF A NEIGHBOR
CAME AND SAID THAT THEY DIDN'T HAVE ANY BREAD, AND THEY WERE TALKING
TO A NEIGHBOR WHO HAD MAYBE A QUARTER, THEY'D GIVE THEM TEN CENTS BECAUSE A
LOAF OF BREAD AT SOME PLACES WAS FIVE CENTS.

A LOT OF PEOPLE USED TO SAY THAT DIXON COURT WAS BAD, BUT THE PEOPLE IN
DIXON COURT DIDN'T THINK SO. THE REPUTATION WAS BAD. I WAS A LITTLE ASHAMED
AT BEING FROM DIXON COURT. I DIDN'T WANT ANYONE TO KNOW. BUT I LOVED
BEING FROM DIXON COURT. I LOVED COMING BACK THERE.

WE DIDN'T VENTURE OFF INTO ALLEYS WE DIDN'T KNOW ANYTHING ABOUT. ALL OF

SOUTHWEST WAS A FAMILY. SO YOU DIDN'T WANT ANYONE TO SAY TO YOUR

PARENTS, "YOU KNOW, I SAW YOUR SON IN SUCH-AND-SUCH A PLACE."

I USED TO BE ASHAMED TO SAY WHERE I WAS FROM. IT WAS HARD . . . BUT I WOULDN'T TRADE ANYTHING FOR THE WAY THAT WE CAME UP. IT MADE ME APPRECIATE SOME OF THE THINGS WE LOOK AT AS A LUXURY TODAY.

THE PEOPLE WHO LIVED IN THE ALLEYS WEREN'T ISOLATED. THEY WERE PART OF OUR

SOCIETY. THIS IS WHAT WE WERE ALL ABOUT. SOME OF THE BEST TIMES THAT I HAD,

I HAD THEM IN THOSE ALLEYS. BACK OFF THE STREET WHERE NOBODY COULD SEE YOU,

YOU COULD DO A LOT OF THINGS THAT YOU COULDN'T DO IN THE STREET.

SWIMMING WAS OFF-LIMITS TO US AS WE KNEW IT. THERE WAS NO SWIMMING POOL. . . .
MOST OF OUR SWIMMING WAS IN THESE KINDS OF PLACES, UP NEAR THE CAPITOL OR OUT
IN THE STREET, OR WE'D GO DOWN TO SPARROWS BEACH OR TO FRANCIS POOL IN FOGGY
BOTTOM. OR WE'D STAND OVER IN UNION STATION WHERE THE WATER WOULD COME
DOWN; THEY'D LET US GO OVER THERE WHEN IT WAS HOT AND GET COOLED OFF.

IT WAS STILL A SEGREGATED CITY, BUT BELIEVE IT OR NOT, THERE WAS MIXED HOUSING.
YOU COULD HAVE HALF A BLOCK THAT WAS WHITE FROM ONE SECTION UP TO THE END,
AND THE NEXT SECTION WOULD BE BLACK FROM ONE END TO THE OTHER.

WE WERE HELD ACCOUNTABLE FOR WHATEVER WE DID. WE WERE ACCOUNTABLE TO OUR
FAMILIES. WE HAD MOTHERS AND FATHERS IN THOSE HOMES. THEY STAYED TOGETHER,
AND THEY ALL HAD VERY STRONG VALUES, AND THE VALUES WERE CONSISTENT.

IN THAT AWFUL PLACE WHERE I LIVED THERE WAS SO MUCH LOVE AND AFFECTION—
NOT JUST IN MY HOUSE BUT IN ALL OF SOUTHWEST. WE HAD A REAL COMMUNITY.

YOU ALMOST HAD TO BE CLOSE TO SURVIVE. NOBODY HAD ANYTHING. WE DIDN'T LOCK

DOORS, NOBODY LOCKED A DOOR. THERE WASN'T ANYTHING FOR ANYBODY TO STEAL.

MY GRANDMOTHER WORKED FOR A DOLLAR A DAY. I'M NOT SURE WHETHER CAR FARE WAS

INCLUDED OR NOT. MAYBE SHE GOT CAR FARE, WHICH WAS TEN CENTS EACH WAY.

AND SHE WOULD GO TO SOME LADY'S HOUSE AND WASH, CLEAN, HELPED HER RAISE

HER CHILDREN. FOR ONE DOLLAR A DAY! BUT WE ATE OFF THAT DOLLAR.

WE DIDN'T GO UPTOWN—DIDN'T NEED TO. THE SCHOOLS WERE DOWN HERE, PLAYGROUNDS
WERE DOWN HERE, MOVIE THEATERS WERE DOWN HERE. GOING UPTOWN WAS QUITE
AN OUTING. YOU DIDN'T NEED TO GO. . . . ESSENTIALLY IT WAS A SMALL TOWN, WITH THE
USUAL IMAGINARY SMALL TOWN VIRTUES AND THE ACTUAL SMALL TOWN VICES.

THAT'S THE WAY WE LIVED DOWN THERE, WITH EXTENDED FAMILIES. IT WAS
PRETTY HARD TO GO HUNGRY, BECAUSE EVERYONE WOULD FEED YOU,
TAKE ANYBODY'S CHILD AND FEED THEM.

I CAN REMEMBER BIG PARTIES. WE USED TO HAVE HALLOWEEN PARTIES WHERE
YOU'D FIND YOURSELF BOBBING FOR APPLES, PARENTS CARRYING YOU FROM HOUSE
TO HOUSE, JUST GETTING IN THE SPIRIT FOR ANYTHING.

MEADOW GOLD—THAT WAS THE FIRST ICE CREAM THAT CAME OUT CHEAP.
UP TILL THEN, ICE CREAM WAS ABOUT THIRTY-FIVE CENTS A PINT. OUT CAME MEADOW
GOLD AT TWENTY CENTS A PINT. WHEN IT MELTED DOWN, IT WAS ALL BUBBLES AND FROTH,
A LOT OF AIR. TWENTY CENTS A PINT, THOUGH.

YOU COULD GO TO THE STORE WITH YOUR BOOK AND GET THINGS WITHOUT
MONEY, AND YOUR FATHER OR MOTHER WOULD PAY AT PAYDAY. I COULD TAKE
MY BOOK DOWN TO THAT CORNER STORE AND GET SOME FOOD, AND
MY MOTHER WOULD COOK IT AND PAY FOR IT LATER.

IT WAS A TOUGH TIME FOR THE KIDS. WHAT WE HAD TO DO AT AN EARLY AGE—I
REMEMBER SO VIVIDLY—WE WENT TO THE WHARF, HELPED SHUCK THE PEAS AND
THE CORN. . . . SOMETIMES WE DIDN'T HAVE MONEY, AND WE'D BE HUNGRY.
SOMETIMES WE USED TO GO DOWN THERE AND TAKE ORANGES AND BANANAS.

I DIDN'T KNOW WHAT A DOOR KEY WAS UNTIL I WAS 16. THERE WAS ALWAYS SOMEONE
HOME ON THE BLOCK. BY THE TIME YOU GOT HOME, THE "INFORMATION BUREAU" WOULD
HAVE COME INTO EFFECT. EVERYBODY CAME TO YOUR DOOR. YOU COULD DO SOMETHING
HERE, BY THE TIME YOU RAN HOME, THEY'D KNOW ABOUT IT.

IN SPITE OF THE CONDITIONS THAT WE LIVED UNDER, THERE WAS GREAT
CAMARADERIE, GREAT TOGETHERNESS. WE GREW UP TOGETHER, WE'RE STILL FRIENDS TODAY,
AND WE REACH OUT TO EACH OTHER, EVEN NOW.

SOME OF THOSE HOUSES NEEDED TO BE REHABILITATED, SOME NEEDED TO BE

REPLACED, AND SOME NEEDED TO BE TORN DOWN, BUT NOT ALL OF THEM. . . .

WHEN THEY GOT THROUGH, EVERYTHING WAS GONE.

THERE WAS THE PROMISE THAT THEY WERE GOING TO GIVE A FACELIFTING TO SOUTHWEST.
THE PEOPLE WERE SENT OUT TO FAR NORTHEAST AND OUT EAST CAPITOL STREET. BUT THEY
NEVER COULD GET BACK, BECAUSE THOSE FAMILIES HAD BEEN OUTPRICED. AND THERE
WASN'T A SOUL WHO THOUGHT THAT WOULD HAPPEN. WE WERE PRETTY NAIVE.

82

THEY DESTROYED A COMMUNITY, A REAL COMMUNITY. IT WAS LIKE A LITTLE

SMALL SOUTHERN TOWN. YOU WILL NEVER FIND THAT KIND OF HISTORY

AGAIN IN WASHINGTON, D.C.

WASHINGTON'S INHABITED ALLEYS

◆ ◆ ◆

"I SHOULD BE HAPPIER IF I KNEW THE ALLEY BILL HAD PASSED."[1]

—FIRST LADY ELLEN AXSON WILSON, ON HER DEATHBED,
AUGUST 5, 1914

"SOUTHWEST HAS BEEN DESTROYED AS THOROUGHLY AS CARTHAGE."[2]

—*WASHINGTON STAR*, 1960

When the wrecking ball finally did its work in the late 1950s, it was the culmination of an effort to eradicate the alleys that had started nearly a century earlier. Residential directories from the 1850s show that some fifty alley enclaves were already in existence throughout the city, probably built by the owners of street-front properties to house servants and laborers in their employ.[3]

Following the Civil War, these cheap dwellings sheltered tens of thousands of emancipated slaves, who flooded into the city from the South. Landowners—realizing the return on their investment would be greater in the densely populated courts than on the surrounding streets—began to construct such houses specifically for the purpose of renting them to the new arrivals. Concentrations sprang up in Northwest, along North Capitol Street and Florida Avenue; in the area known as Foggy Bottom; and in Southwest, a stone's throw from the Capitol.[4]

In fact, the alleys' close proximity to the seat of government—their existence "behind the marble mask" of public Washington—made them a powerful symbol, and a popular target for reformers. One often-told story describes how a local doctor, distressed by the unsanitary conditions, would invite members of Congress to join him on a tour of the alleys. There he would gather them around an outhouse (preferably in the heat of summer, when the effect was most powerful), throw open the door, and say, "Gentlemen, these flies are the same ones that come in your open window and land on your sandwich while you're having lunch on Capitol Hill."

The lawmakers got the message. As early as the turn of the century, Congress was already struggling with what to do about the alley dwellings, which by then were home to nearly 17,000 people—more than 10 percent of Washington's total population.[5] It even enlisted the help of such well-known figures as Jacob Riis, who in the late 1800s had waged war against deplorable slum conditions in New York. Riis visited the capital in 1904 and spoke to members of the Washington Associated Charities about what he had seen. "I am not naturally or easily discouraged," he began. "I am always filled with a notion things will come out right. But I was surprised by the sights I have seen in the national capital. I have been accustomed to see only your handsome blocks, with the look of a holiday city. Today I learned that these very blocks—some within sound of the Capitol, some two squares from Dupont Circle—are rotten inside like a bad apple. . . . Nowhere I have ever been in the civilized world have I seen such a thing as that."[6]

With the election of President Woodrow Wilson in 1913, the cause got a powerful new champion in Ellen Axson Wilson, who pressed her husband to do something about the horrible overcrowding and threat to the public welfare. In September of the following year, Congress passed the Alley Dwelling Act of 1914, in part as a tribute to the first lady, who had died a month earlier. The act made it unlawful to construct any new dwellings in alleys less than 30 feet wide that were not open at both ends; it also required the alleys to be supplied with sewers, water mains, and gas or electric lights.[7]

Though well-intentioned, the provisions were never enforced. Within months, World War I would bring thousands of workers to Washington, making it difficult—not to mention prohibitively expensive—to relocate the alley residents. By the 1930s, the number of inhabited alleys had grown to nearly two hundred. And living conditions had steadily worsened: some 9,000 houses were still lighted by oil lamps, 7,000 were without inside water taps, and 11,000 families had no inside toilets.[8]

In 1934, largely at the urging of another first lady—Eleanor Roosevelt this time—Congress created the Alley Dwelling Authority, charged once and for all with "eliminating the hidden communities in inhabited alleys in the District of Columbia." The target date was set at July 1, 1944, ten years down the road. To speed its task along, the authority was given unprecedented powers (and an initial bankroll of $500,000) to make over at will whole blocks in the District—buy the land, remove the people, and tear down the slums.[9]

Ten years passed—and things hardly changed at all. Fueled by the war effort, Washington's population continued to swell through the

1940s, reaching an all-time high of 800,000 by the end of the decade. In 1945, a year after their supposed demise, the alleys were still teeming with 30,000 residents.[10] Something, it was clear, had to be done.

Congress's answer was to pass the Redevelopment Act of 1945, which gave the capital's planning commission the authority not just to rehabilitate the city's designated "slum areas" but to reconceive entire neighborhoods from the ground up. An independent entity called the Redevelopment Land Agency (RLA) was chartered and given the task of relieving the city of its so-called urban blight. The first area to be targeted for this new form of comprehensive urban renewal: Southwest D.C.

Initially, the agency's intention was to remake Southwest for the benefit of the people who lived there. After all, the thinking went, the area had been a low-income community for so long, and had suffered for so many years with its dismal reputation, that no one else would want to live there anyway. By the early 1950s a plan was devised, and officials set about informing Southwest's residents that they would soon have to move out temporarily in order for their neighborhoods to undergo rehabilitation.

But then a surprising thing happened. Private developers from outside Washington, lured by new federal subsidies available for slum clearance and reconstruction, stepped forward with investment offers that far exceeded the expectations of local planners. Southwest, they insisted, with its scenic riverside location and its proximity to government agencies, could be a showcase community, a vibrant residential neighborhood with the charm of Paris and the cosmopolitan energy of New York. The buildings would be a mix of luxury apartment towers, moderate-income town houses, and government offices; the decaying waterfront would be updated; a sleek new shopping center would replace the rundown storefront markets along the main commercial strip of Fourth Street; and at the heart of a rebuilt Southwest would be a pedestrian plaza and cultural center to rival Venice's Piazza San Marco, complete with sparkling fountains and bustling sidewalk cafes. The potential, the RLA acknowledged—not to mention the long-term boost to city coffers—was too good to pass up. At the time, the

Washington Post hailed the plan as "the most ambitious city rebuilding project ever attempted in America."[11]

Between 1954, when the first alley enclave was demolished, and 1960, when the first high-rises began renting, an entirely different Southwest took shape. All told, 4,500 buildings were torn down, and 23,500 people—77 percent of them black, 64 percent with incomes below the poverty level—were relocated from their homes.[12] In most cases, they moved across the Anacostia River into the Southeast quadrant, and in smaller numbers into Northeast and Northwest. Few ever returned; few could afford to. And, in the end, few wanted to. For the "new" Southwest, while it could boast of being many things, was no longer home.

Five years after the relocation, the Health and Welfare Council of the National Capital Area commissioned a professor of social work, Daniel Thursz, to do a follow-up study of former alley dwellers. "New Southwest may yet develop into the 'Good City,'" he concluded at the time,

> but its birth has been at a cost. It has risen over the ashes of what was a *community* of well-established, though poor, inhabitants. . . . No matter how dirty, inadequate and unsanitary the old Southwest was, it was also *home* for families that had been there a long time. It was the place where parents died, children were conceived and watched as they grew up. It was the site for disputes and occasional celebrations. Its trees, garbage-lined streets and alleys, smells, stores and agencies were all part of a setting that was once familiar to every one of its inhabitants. They walked through the neighborhood with a sense of security and comfort derived in part from the knowledge that behind the weary facades of dilapidated brownstones were friends and acquaintances. . . . For many, the loss was deep and continues to be felt.[13]

James G. Banks was the director of relocation for the RLA, and along with his staff of six was personally responsible for preparing Southwest's residents to move and finding them new places to live—a process that took nearly a decade. "Move means change, and change has fear," he observes. "There were some people who were perfectly able to move and willing to move, and did move even before they were asked to. Because they knew what was coming and they had options. There were some people who had lived [in the alleys] for generations and were just frightened of losing the sense of comfort that they had there."

In retrospect, Banks—a former federal and D.C. housing official, now retired—wonders whether a different approach to redevelopment might not have been in some ways more successful. "If I had it to do over again, I'd do it somewhat differently," he says. "That doesn't mean that we couldn't have made the physical changes. But we could have treated the families in a somewhat different way, helped them if they wanted to rebuild their own houses, or to remodel their own houses. . . . And even if it had taken ten years longer, it would have been worth the time to do it, because what we want to do is to help rekindle the spirit of people, not just to change their physical environment."

In the end, Southwest failed to live up to the grand vision of its planners. Though the area remains an integral part of the city—home to the Smithsonian Institution, the Arena Stage theater, the U.S. Holocaust Memorial Museum, government agencies, congressional office buildings, waterfront seafood restaurants, East Potomac Park, and close to 26,000 people—it has lost much of its essential character as an urban neighborhood. The markets, shops, and social gathering places along Fourth Street have been replaced by a modern though lackluster mall. L'Enfant Plaza, the intended jewel in Southwest's crown, never fully materialized, today housing office buildings and a high-rise hotel instead of the proposed cafes, fountains, and ice-skating rink. Along the residential streets, middle-class apartment towers abut low-income housing projects, and rather than a utopian mix of economic levels, the area remains divided between "haves" and "have-nots." In the words of one longtime resident, who returned to Southwest to live after a twenty-year absence, "All the things that make a living, thriving community are gone, vanished, bulldozed into eternity."[14]

In part because of the lessons learned in Southwest, subsequent redevelopment in Washington was, in fact, carried out differently. In Georgetown, Foggy Bottom, and areas of Capitol Hill, for example, deteriorating neighborhoods were gradually restored and "regentrified." In those areas, too, poor residents were often forced out to make way for others more affluent. But a sense of place was maintained, of history and heritage preserved. "All other sections [of the city] have someplace where you can go back and reconnect about when you were growing up," remarks a Southwest native. "Not a single school that I attended is left."[15]

Even as urban renewal has come to signify a greater emphasis on restoration than on wholesale transformation, debate over the fate of Southwest, and other such crumbling inner-city neighborhoods, continues. While many former residents are quick to acknowledge the benefits that came with improved housing, and the opportunity to raise their children in better circumstances than the ones they knew, they also express bitterness over the loss of their way of life. "They destroyed families. They destroyed a community," says one former resident of Dixon Court. "It wasn't perfect, these people were not rich. But there was a love in that community, a lot of positive things."[16]

Those are the things a camera cannot so readily reveal. It is easy to focus on the eyesores of outhouses and broken-down dwellings; harder to see are the caring bonds forged within those dwellings or the seeds of determination planted there only to flourish years later, far from the harshness of alley life. Just as need and neglect shaped the lives of countless alley children, so too did trusting friendships, supportive families, shared faith, security in a sometimes hostile world—the "positive things" that sustained generations into adulthood, and the things that give any community, even one as impoverished as the alleys of the old Southwest, a richness worth remembering.

NOTES

IN THE ALLEYS

1. James Agee and Helen Levitt, *A Way of Seeing* (Durham: Duke University Press, 1989), p. viii.

2. Dora Bessie Somerville, "A Study of a Group of Negro Children Living in an Alley Culture" (Master's thesis, Catholic University, Washington, D.C., 1941), p. 7.

3. James Borchert, "The Rise and Fall of Washington's Inhabited Alleys: 1852–1972," *Records of the Columbia Historical Society* 48 (1971–72): 268.

4. Daniel Thursz, D.S.W., *Where Are They Now? A Study of the Impact of Relocation on Former Residents of Southwest Washington Who Were Served in an HWC Demonstration Project* (Washington, D.C.: Health and Welfare Council of the National Capital Area, 1966), p. 2.

5. William Stott, *Documentary Expression and Thirties America* (New York: Oxford University Press, 1973), p. 21.

6. Jane Livingston, *The New York School: Photographs 1936–1963* (New York: Stewart, Tabori & Chang, 1992), p. 273.

7. Naomi Rosenblum, "From Protest to Affirmation, 1940–1950," in *Decade by Decade: Twentieth-Century American Photography from the Collection of the Center for Creative Photography,* ed. James Enyeart (Tucson: Center for Creative Photography, University of Arizona, 1989), p. 51.

8. Livingston, *New York School,* p. 274.

9. Beaumont Newhall, "Dual Focus," *Art News* 45, (June 1946): 39.

10. Lawrence Boone, interview with the author, March 18, 1994, Washington, D.C.

11. Princess Whitfield, interview with the author, April 22, 1994, Washington, D.C.

WASHINGTON'S INHABITED ALLEYS

1. Borchert, "Rise and Fall," p. 267. Also Steven J. Diner, *Housing Washington's People: Public Policy in Retrospect,* ed. Steven J. Diner and Helen Young (Washington, D.C.: History and Public Policy Project of the University of the District of Columbia, 1983), p. 10.

2. Harrison M. Ethridge, "Southwest Washington: A Blend of Two Centuries," in *River Park and Its Neighbors—25 Years of Urban Renewal: 1963–1988* (program booklet for the River Park Mutual Homes 25th Anniversary, Washington, D.C., 1988), p. 8.

3. James Ring, "Development of the Inhabited Alleys of Washington" (speech delivered July 3, 1936), Alley Dwelling Authority documents, Washingtoniana Collection, Martin Luther King Jr. Library, Washington, D.C.

4. Borchert, "Rise and Fall," pp. 277–78.

5. James Borchert, "Alley Life in Washington: An Analysis of 600 Photographs," *Records of the Columbia Historical Society* 49 (1973–74): 245.

6. Jacob Riis, speech to the annual meeting of the Associated Charities of Washington, 1904, Alley Dwelling Authority documents, Washingtoniana Collection, Martin Luther King Jr. Library, Washington, D.C.

7. Alley Dwelling Act of 1914, U.S. Laws at Large, vol. 38, part I (Washington, D.C., 1913–15), Alley Dwelling Authority documents, Washingtoniana Collection, Martin Luther King Jr. Library, Washington, D.C.

8. Constance McLaughlin Green, *Washington: A History of the Capital* (Princeton: Princeton University Press, 1976), p. 397.

9. Harold Jones, "Forward Steps," *American City* 49 (December 1934): 67.

10. Elaine B. Todd, "Urban Renewal in the Nation's Capital: A History of the RLA in Washington, D.C., 1946–1973," (Ph.D. diss., Howard University, Washington, D.C., 1986), pp. 41–47.

11. Jeanne R. Lowe, *Cities in a Race with Time: Progress and Poverty in America's Renewing Cities* (New York: Random House, 1967), p. 174.

12. Jerome S. Paige and Margaret M. Reuss, "Safe, Decent and Affordable: Citizen Struggles to Improve Housing in the District of Columbia, 1890–1982," *Housing Washington's People,* p. 91. Also Richard F. Ward, *South and West of the Capitol Dome* (New York: Vantage Press, 1978), p. 73.

13. Thursz, *Where Are They Now?,* pp. 93–101.

14. Paul S. Green, "Old Southwest Remembered: The Photographs of Joseph Owen Curtis," *Washington History* 1 (Fall 1989): 44.

15. Medell Ford, interview with the author, March 19, 1994, Washington, D.C.

16. Lawrence Boone, interview with the author, March 18, 1994, Washington, D.C.

SELECTED REFERENCES

Bicknell, Grace V. *The Inhabited Alleys of Washington, D.C.* Washington: Committee on Housing, Woman's Welfare Department of the National Civic Federation, 1912.

Borchert, James. *Alley Life in Washington: Family, Community, Religion, and Folklife in the City, 1850–1970.* Chicago: University of Illinois Press, 1982.

———. "The Rise and Fall of Washington's Inhabited Alleys." *Records of the Columbia Historical Society* 48 (1971–72): 267–88.

———. "Alley Life in Washington: An Analysis of 600 Photographs." *Records of the Columbia Historical Society* 49 (1973–74): 244–59.

Enyeart, James, ed. *Decade by Decade: Twentieth-Century American Photography from the Collection of the Center for Creative Photography.* Tucson: Center for Creative Photography, the University of Arizona, 1989.

Fant, Barbara. "Slum Reclamation and Housing Reform in the Nation's Capital, 1890–1940." Ph.D. diss., George Washington University, Washington, D.C., 1982.

Groves, Paul A. "The Development of a Black Residential Community in Southwest Washington: 1860–1897." *Records of the Columbia Historical Society* 49 (1973–74): 260–75.

Gutheim, Frederick. *The Federal City: Plans and Realities.* Washington: Smithsonian Institution Press, 1981.

Kaplan, Daile. *Photo Story: Selected Letters and Photographs of Lewis W. Hine.* Washington: Smithsonian Institution Press, 1992.

Lemagny, Jean-Claude, and Andre Rouille. *A History of Photography.* New York: Cambridge University Press, 1987.

Levitt, Helen, and James Agee. *A Way of Seeing.* Durham: Duke University Press, 1989.

Livingston, Jane. *The New York School: Photographs 1936–1963.* New York: Stewart, Tabori & Chang, 1992.

Lowe, Jeanne R. *Cities in a Race with Time: Progress and Poverty in America's Renewing Cities.* New York: Random House, 1967.

Melder, Keith. "Southwest Washington: Where History Stopped." *Washington at Home: An Illustrated History of Neighborhoods in the Nation's Capital,* ed. Kathryn Schneider Smith. Washington: Windsor Publications, 1988.

Newhall, Beaumont. *The History of Photography.* New York: Museum of Modern Art, 1964.

Paige, Jerome S., and Margaret M. Reuss. "Safe, Decent and Affordable: Citizen Struggles to Improve Housing in the District of Columbia, 1890–1982." *Housing Washington's People: Public Policy in Retrospect,* ed. Steven J. Diner. Washington: University of the District of Columbia, 1983.

Rosenblum, Naomi. *A World History of Photography.* New York: Abbeville Press, 1984.

Somerville, Dora Bessie. "A Study of a Group of Children Living in an Alley Culture." Master's thesis, Catholic University, Washington, D.C., 1941.

Stott, William. *Documentary Expression and Thirties America.* New York: Oxford University Press, 1973.

Thursz, Daniel. *Where Are They Now?* Washington, D.C.: Health and Welfare Council of the National Capital Area, 1966.

Todd, Elaine B. "Urban Renewal in the Nation's Capital: A History of the RLA in Washington, D.C., 1946–1973." Ph.D. diss., Howard University, Washington, D.C., 1986.

Weller, Charles Frederick. *Neglected Neighbors: Stories of Life in the Alleys, Tenements and Shanties of the Nation's Capital.* Philadelphia: John C. Winston Co., 1909.

Westerbeck, Colin, and Joel Meyerowitz. *Bystander: A History of Street Photography.* Boston: Little, Brown, 1994.

CREDITS

PAGE 35 (LOWER): Roberta Patrick, interviewed April 15, 1994

PAGES 35 (UPPER), 44, 51, 53, 58 (UPPER), 66, 67: Medell E. Ford,
interviewed March 19, 1994

PAGES 36, 45, 58 (LOWER), 82: Princess D. Whitfield,
interviewed April 22, 1994

PAGE 38 (UPPER): James G. Banks, interviewed May 31, 1994

PAGES 38 (LOWER), 48 (UPPER), 84: Lawrence E. Boone,
interviewed March 18, 1994

PAGES 41, 48: Hilton O. Overton Jr., interviewed October 15, 1993

PAGE 42: Nathaniel Price, interviewed March 10, 1994

PAGE 47: Miles Scott, interviewed April 17, 1994

PAGES 57, 65, 80: Joseph Owen Curtis, interviewed February 27, 1994

PAGE 72: Thomas Fields, interviewed April 23, 1994

PAGE 74: Charles E. Banks, interviewed April 15, 1994

GODFREY FRANKEL

CHRONOLOGY

1912	Born in Cleveland, Ohio
1935	Graduated from Ohio State University, B.A.
1936–43	Wrote and sold advertising for the *Lorain (Ohio) Journal*
	Night club editor of the *Washington Daily News*
1943–44	Photographed alley dwellings in Washington, D.C.
1944	Traveled to New York. Met Alfred Stieglitz, who referred him to Beaumont and Nancy Newhall at the Museum of Modern Art, where his work was subsequently included in two group shows.
1945	Documented the resettlement of Japanese Americans uprooted after Pearl Harbor for the federal War Relocation Authority Program
	Married Lillian Berson, writer, poet, and social worker
1946–50	Moved to New York. Active member of the Photo League, where he chaired and organized the Lewis Hine Collection
1947–49	Documented, as a personal project, storefronts, street scenes, street "furniture," the Third Avenue Elevated, and people on the Lower East Side of Manhattan

1950	Graduated from Columbia University School of Social Work, M.S.W.
1950–62	Administered Jewish Community Center programs, Cleveland Heights, Ohio
1954	Wrote *Short Cut to Photography* (Sterling Publishing Co.), cited "best of year" by the *New York Times* for photo books for youth
1962–82	Appointed senior consultant, National Institute on Drug Abuse, U.S. Public Health Service, Rockville, Maryland
1980	Organized and directed crisis intervention centers for Cuban Mariel refugees
1980–86	Appointed visiting professor in community development and organization behavior, University of Maryland, College Park
1982	Retired from federal government
1988	Completed Fine Arts degree, University of Maryland, College Park

SELECTED INDIVIDUAL EXHIBITIONS

1995   George Hemphill Fine Arts Gallery, Washington, D.C.

1993   Vision Gallery, San Francisco, California

1992   Kathleen Ewing Gallery, Washington, D.C.

1990   Middendorf Gallery, Washington, D.C.

1987   Middendorf Gallery, Washington, D.C.

1985   Montgomery College Photo Gallery, Rockville, Maryland

1977   Neikrug Galleries, New York

1971   B'nai B'rith Klutznick Gallery, Washington, D.C.

1969   American Institute of Architects, Washington, D.C.

1951   Jewish Community Center, Cleveland, Ohio (joint show with
        Roman Vishniac)

1949   Museum of the City of New York

SELECTED GROUP
EXHIBITIONS

1994	Corcoran Gallery of Art, Washington, D.C.
1993–94	George Hemphill Fine Arts, Washington, D.C.
1992	Kathleen Ewing Gallery, Washington, D.C.
1989	Middendorf Gallery, Washington, D.C.
	Arts Club of Washington, D.C., "Ten Washington Photographers"
1986	National Museum of American Art, Washington, D.C.
1973	Midtown Y.M.H.A., New York
1959	George Eastman House, Rochester, New York, "Photography at Mid-Century"
1944–56	Cleveland Museum of Art, Annual May Show
1946–48	Museum of Modern Art, New York, circulating exhibition throughout the United States and Canada
1948	Museum of Modern Art, New York, "In and Out of Focus"
1946	Museum of Modern Art, New York, "New Photographers"

SELECTED COLLECTIONS

1994   Cleveland Museum of Art

        Japanese American National Museum, Los Angeles, California

        University of Maryland, Baltimore County, Photo Collections

        Yale University Art Gallery, New Haven, Connecticut

1992   Baltimore Museum of Art

        Houston Museum of Fine Arts

        Syracuse University Art Collection, Syracuse, New York

1988   YIVO Institute for Jewish Research, New York

1987   Hallmark Photo Collection, Kansas City, Missouri

1986   Colorado Historical Society, Georgetown, Colorado

1985   Museum of Modern Art, New York

        National Museum of American Art, Washington, D.C.

1983   Corcoran Gallery of Art, Washington, D.C.

1949   New York Public Library Folk Art Project, New York
        Museum of the City of New York